A Pocket Full of Poetry

C J Reilly

BookLeaf Publishing

Presentation by *BookLeaf Publishing*

Web: www.bookleafpub.com

E-mail: info@bookleafpub.com

ISBN: 9789357618298

First edition 2022

This little collection is of course dedicated to the man who has been by my side cheering me on since the beginning of time. My Husband, my soul mate and so much more. There aren't the words but he knows ♥

ACKNOWLEDGEMENT

Thank you to all who have encouraged me and gee'd me on over the years to do something with my writing. From many years ago, up until the present day I have had so much amazing feedback and every single little bit has been appreciated and remembered.

Special thanks to my youngest daughter who innocently told me she couldn't wait for me to die so that she could finally have a good look through my many notebooks! I was of course horrified but it hit home. We only live once! So Hazel feel free to have a rummage anytime and thanks again for inadvertently making me shift my arse!

PREFACE

An eclectic collection of some of my work so far.............

I have scoured my collection, finished some pieces, and gathered together what I hope will be an enjoyable selection of poetry for everyone.
I have only included one piece that is truly personal to me and I have left it till last.
Read from the front page through to the back cover or dip in and out as you like.
There aren't many rules when writing poetry and there are fewer when reading.
Just enjoy.

The Tips of My Toes

I push myself up
With the tips of my toes
Through the air, to the clouds
Wayheyhey here I go
I have no propeller
No jetpack, no wings
Who need them when dreams
Are such wondrous things
There's nothing can stop me
From flying away
I don't want to come down
So up here I will stay
It's peaceful and warm
Way up here in the sky
There is nothing quite like
Being able to fly
I hover about
At the tops of the trees
Then I soar to the stars
Just by bending my knees
I travel so fast
Over cities and towns
When I see somewhere nice
I will float gently down
I'll have an ice-cream

Then I'll rest for a while
When it's time to go home
I'll set off with a smile
I push myself up
With the tips of my toes
Through the air, back to bed
Wayheyhey, here I go

Drowned Village, The Ballad of Bothwellhaugh

It was torn to the ground
So the old story goes
But no amount of dynamite
Could bury the ghosts
A part of our history
Suspended in time
Buried under the water
On top of the mine

Now it's bathed in darkness
Too deep to catch the sun
But the spirit of Bothwellhaugh
Carries on

To this very day
The spirits remain
They dance in the moonlight
And kiss in the rain
Magical orbs
Laughing silently
While the rain hits the water
So quietly

Now it's bathed in the darkness

Too deep to catch the sun
But the spirit of Bothwellhaugh
Carries on

Imaginations captured
Minds delving in the past
The spirit of this mining town
Will always last
To this very day
The ghosts never leave
Under the surface
Under the breeze

Bathed in eternal darkness
Too deep to catch the sun
The memory of Bothwellhaugh
Will always carry on

The 80s Flashback

Bleached blonde hair
Big dark roots
Rah Rah skirts
Chelsea boots
Dungarees
Kylie dresses
Jelly shoes
Backcombed tresses
Eyeliner black
Lipstick red
Relax don't do it
Frankie said
Runny mascara
Cheap fake tan
George Michael
I'm Your Man
Neon sandals
The Hit Parade
Long Hot Summer
Live Aid
Like A Virgin
Crazy for You
Who's That Girl?
Singing True Blue
Space invaders

Rubik's cube
Top of the Pops
And The Tube
Adam Ant
Prince Charming
The Breakfast Club
Pretty In Pink
Culture Club
Bronski Beat
Dr Martins
Stomping feet
ZX Spectrum
Charts on tape
INXS
Paula Yates
Roller skates
Disco dancing
Dangly earrings
Freddy prancing
Tizwas, Swap Shop
3, 2, 1
People winning
Dusty Bin
Metal Mickey
Channel Four
Brookside Close
Orinoco Flow
Pedal pushers
Sun in Spray

God Save the Queen
Morrissey
Back To the Future
Marty McFly
Bros said
Drop The Boy
Sam Fox
Smash Hits
T J Hooker
Aerosmith
Reebok high-tops
Flash Dance
Leg warmers
Wrist bands
Steve Strange
New romance
Synthesiser
Birdy Dance
My Little Pony
Roland Rat
He-man, She-ra
Thunder Cat
Game of Life
Buckaroo
Operation
Guess Who
Jackie, Debbie
Bunty, Mandy
Beano, Buster

Twinkle, Dandy
Roger Rabbit
Uncle Buck
Beetle juice
Howard Duck
Freddy Krueger
Halloween
Childs Play
Friday Thirteen
Michael Jackson
Moonwalking
Hong Kong Phooey
Kung foo fighting
Casio keyboard
Speak n Spell
Spiro-graph
Fashion Wheel
Penelope Pitstop
Why Don't You
Blanket Blank
Give Us a Clue
Sheena Easton
Morning Train
Jason and Kylie
Scott and Charlene
Tracy Chapman
Fast Cars
Topgun
Star Wars

Sony Walkman
Ghetto blaster
Magna Doodle
View Master
Creamola foam
Caramac
Mister Frosty
Crackerjack
Cabbage Patch Kid
Soda Streams
Weird Science
Electric Dreams
Rainbow Brite
Banana Splits
12" Vinyl
Polaroid pics
Ripped jeans
Crimped hair
Tiny Tears
Care Bear
Strawberry Shortcake
Chelsea Whoppers
Lemon Popsicle
Gob Stoppers
Debbie Gibson
Tiffany
Gregory's Girl
Stand By Me
Mister T

The A Team
3D glasses
Were red and green
Jamie and His
Magic Torch
Ferris Bueller's
Day Off
Gummy Bears
Glow Worm
Debbie Harry
Paul Young
Shakin' Stevens
This Ole House
Garfield Cat
Danger Mouse
Salt n Pepa
Eternal Flame
Five Star
Purple Rain
Bungle, Zippy
George and Geoffrey
Aunty Jane
Rod and Freddy
Opel Manta
Ford Capri
Parachute pants
Stiletto heels
Brat pack
Pac-man

Gremlins
Super Gran
Neon beads
Button Moon
Ah, the 80's
Gone to soon <3

Four Seasons

We lay together, bathing in the mid-day sunshine.
No worries, no fears, just an almost overwhelming feeling of completeness and contentment.
If we had known then what we know now would we have held on tighter to those moments?
Would we have been more reluctant to let them go? Probably.

They slipped away from us all too easily.

They slipped away into the glaring autumn sun, coupled with the cooling breeze.
No more were our days filled with the pleasant sensation of our skins absorbing the afternoon sun.
Our fading tans were covered up with heavier fabrics designed to keep the heat in and the chill out.

The summer, while seeming endless at the time, had blended all too quickly into Autumn.
We walked together, hands entwined, making casual observations not only about our dour

surroundings but about the multitude of strangers passing us by.

"Do you think they're a couple?" You asked me, one eyebrow raised at the obvious age gap of the young gentleman and his elderly lady companion.

"Nah, that'll be his Granny, he's clearly taking her for a wee stroll." I responded, unable to imagine them as anything more.

The young man, at that precise moment, chose to prove me wrong as he bent slightly and kissed his lady friend tenderly on the lips.

"Ah I was right, he's her toy boy. I wouldn't mind a sugar mama!" you teased.

I squeezed your fingers tightly, feeling the familiar sting of irrational jealousy in my heart.

If I'd known then what I know now, would I have reacted the same way? Probably.

Autumn with its dark mornings and darker nights melded into Winter without us noticing the changes.

Without warning we were donning woollen hats, scarves, and mittens to ward off the numbness.

Our walks were brisker.

We had less time to play our people watching games, our heads often kept down in an attempt to keep our faces from freezing.

If we had known then what we know now,
would we have slowed down?
Would we have tried harder to savour every moment? Probably.

Spring has sprung and as I embrace the first warm day of the year, alone, I wish I'd known.

Fairy Dust

Fairy wings
So soft and light
You can barely see them
When she takes flight

Perfect features
Big blue eyes
She flutters her eyelids
As she takes to the skies

Dazzling smile
Teeth shiny white
When she opens her mouth
She lights up the night

Fairy dust
Sprinkled around
Watch as it falls
And lands on the ground

If you are lucky
And some lands on you
Close your eyes, make a wish
And your wish will come true

A Cats Life

I open my eyes
When I hear the sound
Of someone's footsteps
Outside on the ground

My human is coming
And that means food
And maybe some milk
A cat's life is good

I'll just lie still
And pretend I don't see
Then she'll come over
And fuss over me

I roll myself around
Onto my back
She scratches the right bits
She sure has the knack

Mmmm yummy yum
I can smell fish
I think I'll get up
And empty my dish

Now I am thirsty
Time for some milk
Then I’ll clean my fur
Till it's soft as silk

My human is sat now
With a nice cup of tea
I’ll go and annoy her
And let her pet me

What Would he Say

I wonder what he'd say to me
If only he could talk
"Is it time for dinner yet?"
Or "Take me for a walk"

Imagine how much simpler
My wee dog's life would be
If he could talk instead of bark
And have a chat with me

He'd tell me when he's hungry
And when he needed out
He'd tell me if he's lonely
He'd tell me not to shout

If my dog could talk to me
And understand when I replied
He'd know how much I loved him
Until the day he died

The Staffy Curse

It is not me
I am not bad
These misconceptions
Make me mad

The media frenzy
Blame the breed
The Staffy curse
Is sad to read

They don't report
The positive things
The love we give
The joy we bring

We might be strong
And made of muscles
But we love our hugs
And playful tussles

We are devoted
With massive hearts
We run away from
Our smelly farts

If you know
A Staffy well
You will understand
My need to tell

We are not monsters
We are not evil
We are not savage
Or dogs of the devil

We are quite simply
Man’s best friend
Loyal and true
Right till the end

Death Row

I stand here in this concrete square
With wire mesh all around
I'm just a lonely puppy dog
Who's stuck here in the pound

I don't know what I ever did
That my humans thought so wrong
I've always been a good girl
I've been stuck in here so long

People come and look at me
They pause then walk on by
Every time they walk away
It makes me want to cry

I only have a few more days
To find my forever home
If no one comes to save me
I will die here all alone

I promise to behave myself
To be loyal, faithful and true
I'll never ever let you down
I'm the perfect dog for you

Always The Good

I can't get the concept
Straight in my head
One minute we're breathing
Next minute we're dead

Just one split second
To snuff out a life
A brother, son or husband
A sister, a daughter, a wife

I know we all get older
I accept that we all die
And if it's our time
I don't question why

The thing about dying
That makes me so sad
Is it's often the good
And rarely the bad

Lovely To See You

You come to me
In the dead of night
While I'm sound asleep
It's lovely to see you
Even though it's surreal
More memories to keep

After you've been
The things that you said
Stay with me all day
I wish when I woke
You were still there
And hadn't gone away

It's not just you
Who visits my dreams
There are lots of others to
But none of those mean
As much to me
As my visits from you do

Somebody's There

My scalp starts to tingle
There's a draught in the air
The temperature drops
I know somebody's there

I see a dark shadow
From the side of my eye
It's the spirits that linger
Long after they die

The atmosphere's eerie
Though they mean me no harm
They confirm they are there
With a touch on my arm

They've just come to visit
They're not here to stay
I ask them politely
If they've something to say

Most tell me their secrets
Some don't make a sound
But they all seem quite happy
Just floating around

When I Look In The Mirror

When I look in the mirror
It looks just like my face
But who is that girl
Standing there in my place

When I look in the mirror
Who's the girl that I see
I know on the surface
She looks just like me

When I look in the mirror
I examine her closely
And I scare myself silly
'Cause I think she looks ghostly

When I look in the mirror
I wonder what I would do
If she jumped out and grabbed me
Or shouted out BOOOO!

Another World

Beyond the realms of normality
There lies another world
A supernatural spiritual reality
Is beginning to unfurl

They can walk on our ground
But we can't step on theirs
We'll never know where it is found
And most of us don't care

Who wants to meet the undead
The spirits or the fae
We're safer in our own bed
To live another day

Even though we're kept away
Our paths are bound to meet
In still of night or light of day
They're wandering our streets

The vamps stand watch outside our homes
Unable to come in
But the spirits, fairies, and the gnomes
Can enter anytime

Some of them are wicked
And some are just divine
But whether they are bad or good
They send shivers down your spine

Cold Bloodied Friends

In the still of the moonlit night
Nothing is moving, no one's in sight
But things are never quite as they seem
When the world falls asleep, dreaming her
dream

When we are all sound asleep in our bed
While the sheep are jumping around in our head
Outside in the cities, the villages, and towns
Our cold bloodied friends are prowling around

First comes the hunt and with it the thrill
Then comes the chase, then it's in for the kill
When they've finished their meal, the burning
has gone
Dispose of the corpse and it's time to move on

After the feed, the fangs will retract
They can mingle with ease and no fear of attack
Plenty of time for a club and a bar
That nobody notices is truly bizarre

They're eccentric, outrageous. Not known to be
shy

They can muddle your thoughts with a look in the eye
When the stars disappear, and the moon starts to fade
There is only one rule that can't be disobeyed

Before the sun rises and lights up the sky
They must be in their coffins or else they will fry
So later tonight when you're safe in your bed
Don’t bother with sheep, count vampires instead

If one comes a knocking
Just remember two things
Stay in your bed
And don’t invite him in!

Waiting For Dark

Finally the sun is setting
Out of this coffin I am getting
Been lying straight as a rod all day
Waiting for nightfall, my time to play

It's just as well I feel no pain
Or I would never move again
My joints would seize, my bones would ache
My neck would hurt, my back would break

I lift the lid and jump out fast
It's good to have a stretch at last
I make my coffin and close it tight
And make my way into the night

The moon is out, it's time to feed
To catch a human and make them bleed
The dregs of society are no good
Their tainted blood won't pass for food

So I hunt for a maiden who's all alone
Or a gent who is walking on his own
Their blood is my life force you see
And simply put, it's them or me

Who's that up there on the road ahead
It's such a shame he'll end up dead
I swoop down from my hiding place
And see the terror on his face

He has no time to run or shout
I have him now, my fangs are out
I bare his neck and take a bite
He's passed out, must have been the fright

I drink until I've drained him dry
Then leave him on the road to die
My thirst is quenched, my hunger abated
My belly is full, my appetite sated

I'm free now to do whatever I like
Until the sun rises and it's no longer night
As soon as dawn breaks, at the sound of the lark
I'm back in my coffin, waiting for dark

One Small Bite

Emergence from dark skies to dawn
As the sun climbs up the sky
As night turns into summer’s morn
A tear spills from my eye

For with the daylight and the sun
The dark ones hide away
They cannot join in with the fun
In darkness they must lay

If only the moon stayed in the sky
And the sun only shone from noon
My love would have longer by my side
Still morning comes too soon

For now and all of eternity
Or until the day I die
I'll sit here waiting patiently
For my one true love to rise

I hope and pray he'll take me
I'd gladly give my life
Just one small bite is all I need
To become his vampire wife

The Secret

The big house
Sits on its own
Nothing nearby
It's all alone
Up the path
At the top of the stair
Stands the doorway
Looming there
Through the porch
Into the hall
The cellar door is
On the faraway wall
Down the stairs
Behind the door
In the cellar
Under the floor
Lies a secret
Never to be told
Not for money
Not for gold
Don't tell a person
Don't say a word
Don't utter a sound
Lest you be heard
It's lain down there

For many a year
Buried deep
And many fear
That one day soon
This thing will rise
Climb out of its grave
And open its eyes
Those who know
Hope and pray
That in the ground
This thing will stay
With the dirt packed tight
And a cross on top
A bolted door
Designed to stop

Next time you see
A house on its own
Nothing nearby
Standing alone
Stay clear of the path
Don't climb the stair
Don't chap the door
That's looming there
Don't go through the porch
Or into the hall
Stay away from the door
On the faraway wall
If you don't listen

If you don’t heed
I can almost be certain
You’ll end up DEID!

*DEID - Scottish vernacular for dead.

Oh Angel

Oh angel, shine your guiding light
I really need your help tonight
It's all gone wrong, nothing's right
Please angel with your halo bright

Oh angel, lend a helping hand
I know you'll help me if you can
There's no one else, no back-up plan
No one cares or understands

Find my Mummy, she's gone away
My daddy's gone to jail to stay
I have no toys, no games to play
I've not had much to eat today

I'm in this house, all on my own
I get so scared when I'm alone
Please angel bring my Mummy home
I promise not to cry or moan

Oh angel, shine your guiding light
I really need your help tonight
I know that you can make things right
Please angel, with your halo bright

Egg Shells

Your dinner's out
It's on the table
I never see it coming
I am unable
To tell exactly
When the next blow will come
It's nothing I've said
It's nothing I've done

I'm walking on eggshells
Trying to read the mood
A drawn out silence
Is never good
I always do
The best I can
Nothing seems to
Please this man

He's always looking
For the slightest wrong
If I look the wrong way
Or sing the wrong song
There's never a method
Behind his madness
He's just no good

And full of badness

I really should
Defend myself
It's up to me
And no one else
One day soon
My mind will break
I'll take no more
For pity's sake

But I guess
That for just now
I'll carry on
Not take a bow
For when his
Final curtain falls
He won't see it coming
I'll cut off his balls

Three Wishes Each

Dad and I both had three wishes each

We didn't know whether to use them or keep

A hold of them to use them over the years

We thought we may need them when hard times were near

I made my first wish and got my first baby boy

When he arrived both our hearts filled with joy

We knew there and then what our wishes were for

We'd spread them out nicely and wish for five more

It was Dads turn to use one of his wishes next

He wished for a brother for Scott, one just like his

A brother arrived and our hearts filled with love

For this tiny wee boy who came out with one shove

We had two wee boys now, so close to each other

It was my turn to wish again so I wished for another

I wished for a baby, not fussed either way

And along came a wee bruiser who melted both our hearts that day

Well soon it was time for Dads second wish

He closed his eyes and pictured Scott with three brothers just like his

But when Chrissy was born both our hearts skipped a beat

He was so small and fragile, maybe not ours to keep

But he was a wee fighter, and he held his own

And it wasn't too long before he was home

It was my turn to wish, and I was feeling left out

So, I wished for a daughter to help me sort these boys out

My wish came true, and we had a beautiful baby girl

Who certainly made an entrance into this world

The minute we seen her it was love at first sight

We knew our boys would protect her with all of their might

The time had come for dad to use up his last wish

And he wished the hardest he ever had wished

He wished for his dad to get better and not die

But he knew as he wished with a tear in his eye

His wish couldn't come true, it was already too late

But something happened that day, let's just call it fate

Because nine months later our last child was born

Another beautiful girl and her Grandad lives on

We all know our Hazel has been here before

Dads wish had came true, we couldn’t have asked for more

We used all our wishes to make our big family

And neither of us would have it any other way

Yes, sometimes it’s hard, but the good outweighs the bad

Looks like we did alright, me and your Dad.......

www.ingramcontent.com/pod-product-compliance
Lightning Source LLC
Chambersburg PA
CBHW062203160726
48282CB00027B/969
* 9 7 8 9 3 5 7 6 1 8 2 9 8 *